I CAN'T DO IT! Why did I say yes?

Powerful Presence for Performers, Teachers and Public Speakers

Britt Forsberg

Thank you Rick!

I CAN'T DO IT! Why did I say yes?
First edition 2017

Published by Britt Forsberg

Artworker Jordan Uwins

ISBN 978-1-5262-0623-7

About Britt

Britt is from Gävle in Sweden and has been living in Brighton, England since 1994.

Involved with performing since she was seven, she has worked extensively as an actor, director and teacher of voice, movement, acting technique, presentation skills and confidence building.

She has Diplomas in Physical Theatre and Theatre Leadership and has attended the Grotowski Institute in Wroclaw, Poland.

She has founded theatre companies in Sweden and England and for the last 25 years, has devoted herself to adapting and refining her unique and highly effective acting techniques to work for people from all walks of life and in all sorts of situations. Hundreds of actors, singers, performers and public speakers from as far and wide as Stockholm, New York, Madrid and London now use Britt's techniques to improve their skills and to... shine on stage!

Her methods are a must for anyone wanting to develop good communication skills, self-confidence and well-being.

For people who present
or want to or have to or dream of or simply should

Words I use in the book

To make my explanations as simple as possible,
I regularly use the following words:

Presenter
Anyone who is going to be in front of a group of people to present
something, e.g. an actor, performer, teacher or public speaker.

Presentation
Anything that any of the above is presenting i.e. a part in a play,
a song, a speech, lesson, lecture or a sermon.

Audience
Those who will be listening to and seeing the presentation.

Stage
The area from which the presenter makes his/her presentation.

Auditorium
The area where the audience is situated.

Chapters

It's like...you and I are sitting in a café.
I tell you a few things that I have discovered.
I scribble them down on a napkin.
And push it over to you.

This book is that napkin.

Chapter 1
Why are you a presenter?

Question the ultimate reason

Reflect Upon **Why are you a presenter?**

Because you chose it?

Because someone else chose it for you?

Because you have to?

Why?

Because you love performing?

You have to do presentations at work?

You are a teacher?

You have been asked to give a speech?

You want to be a star?

Reflect upon **Why should we do live presentations?**

Why should we drag ourselves away from the comfort of our own homes or the convenience of our workplaces where we can receive information through our smart phones, internet or TV?

Well, there are a few things that only live presenting can deliver:

Energy – given
and received.
To be energised.

Real connections - to be
seen, to be heard, to listen
and to be listened to, to feel
understood, to feel special.

Presence – in life, with life, with everybody.

With everything...

GOOD NEWS!

You are not selected to be on stage because you
are necessarily better than everybody else.

You don't have to prove anything.

Because...

It's not actually about you!

It is about "the message"
and it is about the audience.

You are the person who this time happens to be the one who shall deliver the presentation.

You only have to allow
the message to flow through you.

And then flow into the audience...

...into each person in the audience...

THAT IS A NICE WAY

TO ACT

TO SING

TO PRESENT

TO DANCE

TO PERFORM

TO TEACH

TO PREACH

TO BE

ONLY THEN WILL

your ACTING TAKE US ON A JOURNEY

your SINGING TOUCH OUR SOUL

your PRESENTATION INSPIRE US TO ACTION

your DANCE SWEEP OUR EMOTIONS

your PERFORMANCE TICKLE OUR SENSES

your TEACHING REACH US

your PREACHING OPEN US

your BEING MAKE US FEEL LOVED

Chapter 2
Why do presence training?

From "Yes!" to "I'm an idiot!"

Emotions are really unreliable. One day you say yes to something and feel great about it. Another day you wonder what planet you were on that day...

Reflect upon **Something like this happens to you:**

Your boss asks if you can do a presentation at work.

You join a theatre group and a lovely part is offered to you.

Your local charity needs a compere for a fundraising event.

Your friend asks if you can be best man at his wedding.

You have a calling and want to share your message.

You think something like:

   – Alright then, if they think I'm the right person.

You say: Yes!

...and...

Sometime later...

You are busy:

Preparing your presentation.

Learning your script.

Organising your lesson.

Practising your song.

Formulating your speech.

...the day of your presentation is getting closer...

Is this you?

LEARN LEARN LEARN LEARN
-Ouch!

TRYING TO SLEEP SLEEP SLEEP
-Oh... now I CAN'T sleep!

WORK BUILDING UP

I can't focus on anything.

EGO PLAYING UP

- Can you be quiet please!

-sorry
- sorry
- sorry

RELATIONSHIPS SUFFER

TENSION

- I can't wait for it to be over.

WISHING FOR THE FUTURE
TO ARRIVE QUICKLY = future as in AFTER the event.

16

... and is this how your days start to look?

I CAN'T DO IT!

Why did I say yes?

I'm an idiot!

WHO DO I THINK I AM?
I don't know anything about anything.
By the way, all the people I work with
are stupid or better than me!

*If you are doing this to your body, voice and soul, you
are going to find it hard to get the best from yourself
at all, let alone when you present something.*

Let us start again...so...

You have been given the opportunity to be in front of an audience?

 – Yeah?

CONGRATULATIONS! MAKE THE MOST OF IT!

 – Huh, easy for you to say!

Because your presence can have a positive and lasting effect on your audience.

 – But I am so nervous... I'll be absolutely hopeless!

Look, first of all you've got to realise that...

We in the audience are not concerned about your worries.

We are not interested in your ego.

We are actually interested in ourselves!

I am interested in myself when I go to receive a presentation.

Do I want to sit in the audience and be judging you?
Is my main reason for being there to decide if:
You are bad? ...or... You are good?

No it's not... I'm there because...

I want to learn from your subject.

I want to listen to your speech.

I want to receive information from your presentation.

I want to go on a journey with you when you perform.

I want to be inspired.

PRESENCE IN HEAD →

Yes, but I have to remember what to say. And I look awful! By the way, I've been told to pretend that the audience is naked. That's going to be difficult!

I'm so afraid of making mistakes so I have to think of what I'm doing next all the time...
what AM I doing next ???
Oh no, I can't remember!
You see !!!

This is your insecurity talking.
You are worried about not being good enough.
You think the audience will be judging you.
We often say that this is your ego taking over.

What is ego?

"Ego is your consciousness of your own identity"

The greater the ego, the looser the connection with other people and your surroundings and the harder it will be for you to enjoy the journey ...and to shine!

Your ego will take over when you are too much in your head and have very little presence in your body.

If you are too much in your head – this might happen: LOOK!

There is no opening out. You run the risk of feeling stuck! And lonely...

You need to work from an ego-free place.

— What?
I don't know what you are talking
about! I'm really busy now.
If you'll excuse me, I have a lot to do.
I have to learn an awful lot of text
and lose weight!
I don't have time for this...

Yes, but how is the audience going to
receive anything special if it comes from
a place of excessive self-criticism
...worries...doubts and stress?

` Oh?

25

WELL, everything has got its time:

You do need to learn, practise and own your material but... meanwhile, you need to make time to work on yourself so that you can become an ego-free presenter.

To help create an ego-free zone for when you practise (and when you present) your material, you need to let go of your private present mood state.

Let me explain why...

You are just about to prepare and practise your material...
and this happens:

 — I'm not feeling too good today. I had a stressful conversation with somebody earlier.

Your present mood state is affected by what happened earlier.

 — I can't stop thinking about it and I feel bad.

You are clinging on to the feelings from that conversation.

 — I must start concentrating on my work!

You are trying to force yourself to get into your work with the intrusive thoughts clinging on to you!

I can't concentrate.
I'm stupid.
Get focused!
I can't remember anything!

You're trying to do two things at the same time...go over your bad feelings and practise your presentation.

I'm sick and tired of my work, it's stressful and I'm so tired.

It's really tiring splitting yourself in half.

I'm calling in sick tomorrow.

...so you end up not giving your work a chance to live.

You need to choose:

Are you going to practise your material or
are you going to deal with whatever is on your mind?

If your answer is:

I want to practise my material; I want to do my best and
I will deal with my feelings another time.

Great!

Then use the techniques

in the next chapter to help you to:

Let go of your private present mood state.

Chapter 3
Presence training

Be present in body and soul

Reflect upon **See yourself as an instrument**

Your body, with your voice and inner self is the instrument that you will be using to do your presentation. The first step is to become really present with your instrument and then to clean and then tune it so it plays the purest sound.

EXERCISE STAND IN NEUTRAL

Stand with feet hip-width apart.

Keep your legs straight but don't lock your knees.

Let your arms and hands hang down by your sides and relax hands and fingers.

In this way, you start to reduce what your "private you" wants to do.

Achieved presence →

— still can't stop thinking about it.

Presence is still only in the head and probably in the upper chest.

Presence level

EXERCISE **BREATHE IN AND SIGH X 3**

Stand in neutral.

Take a deep, generous breath in and sigh.

A proper sigh. One that you really mean… just let it out!

Do this three times and allow a bigger sound on the third one.

Presence level increases

aah… 'nice

You should feel better because you've let go of what was occupying you.

not far to go now

This has brought the presence down to approximately the top of your legs.

EXERCISE **DROP-A-LEVEL**

Now...let go of the air in your lungs as if you puncture them.

Let your weight - the whole of you - drop down into your body.

As if you completely "give up".

all the way to your feet

presence

- I feel like I have landed in myself.

I feel calm and I feel good.

Yes you have landed in yourself. Yes, it is surprisingly calm in there when we "let go".

— I'm not too bad.
I'm an ok person.

This is who I am! This is me! This is my instrument!

Result So by DROPPING–A–LEVEL,
you relax into your instrument,
into everything that's there.

Reflect upon So what's there?

Inside your body? Inside your instrument?

Well, there are the memories of the many experiences in your life and the feelings they evoke.

Some are self-lived, some are feelings you have received from other people.

And some are emotions you have encountered by watching a film for example.

Feelings and memories useful for your presentation are also there.

Result **"Breathe in and sigh"** and **"Drop-a-level"**
will help you to gain access to these useful feelings. And by
drawing on feelings from within your body (rather than
being stuck in your head), will help you to communicate with
more authenticity.

Presence in body achieved!
Still to do: Be present with your surroundings...

Be present with your surroundings

Reflect upon Do not judge your surroundings

Is this you?

It is so easy to get carried away with thoughts and feelings connected to items around us. They can hijack our attention and easily distract us from what we should/would like to focus on.

Remember, you need to keep your instrument clean and open.

EXERCISE **LOOK AT YOUR SURROUNDINGS WITHOUT JUDGING**

Breathe in and sigh x 3.

Drop-a-level.

Look at an item in the room for approximately 3 seconds.

Look at it FOR REAL, make sure you really see it.

Look at another three items in your surroundings in the same way.

Look at different spots on the walls, the ceiling and the floor in the same way. Or if outdoors, look at any points that are easy to focus on including in the sky.

Let the item or spot in through your eyes, without attaching any particular opinions or thoughts to it.

Do all of this with full concentration for a minimum of 1-2 minutes.

Then...do it for as long and as often as you wish...

Result Look how calm the room is now

You might find that it is hard to avoid attaching opinions about items and surroundings. But if you exercise your eyes in this way regularly you will become better and better at it. You will notice that you become calmer and more present in the space you're in.

You will also notice more things and live more in the HERE and NOW.

EXERCISE **LISTEN TO YOUR SURROUNDINGS WITHOUT JUDGING**

Focus on your ears and listen without attaching any particular thoughts to what you hear for 1-2 minutes.

Listen to all the sounds:
The quiet ones, the loud ones and even listen to the silence...

With an "open listening" you will become more alert and sensitive to what is happening around you.

This will help you to decide whether to react or not to react to those sounds.

Exercise "Looking at and Listening to your surroundings without judging" whenever you have an opportunity.

You can do this at home, at work or pretty much anywhere.

Be prepared for peaceful surprises...

Be present with people

The same applies to your relationship with people
Look at the pictures and spot the difference:

Picture no 1

Picture no 2

Answer **The difference between the pictures is**

PICTURE no. 1

PEOPLE ARE JUDGING EACH OTHER

This is very tiring and it lowers the confidence of both the person judging and the person being judged. You need to judge people sometimes to avoid getting into trouble, but most everyday judging is unnecessary and only blocks us from really meeting each other. Subconsciously, we often judge other people because we are worried about them judging us.

So who started?

We don't need to know that. We only need to understand that if one stops, the other one is less likely to do it.

You can be the one stopping!

PICTURE no. 2

PEOPLE ARE NOT JUDGING EACH OTHER

Can you see how much space there is around them? Because the tiring activity of judging has been removed, there is space for other possibilities. This raises the confidence of all involved. It is truly wonderful to interact with people who do not form meaningless personal opinions, for example about what we wear or what we look like. We are so much more than what we look like at first glance.

Give each other a chance to be.

After you have looked at your surroundings without judging, look at people in the same way.

EXERCISE **LOOK AT PEOPLE WITHOUT JUDGING**

Look at a person for approximately 5 seconds.

Look at the person for real.

Make sure you really see him/her.

Let in what you see without attaching any particular opinions, thoughts or judgements.

If there are several people available to look at, do this exercise for approximately 1 minute.

You can obviously carry on looking at people in this way, now and again throughout the day...

Those you look at can be people in the street, on the bus or in the same room.

They don't need to be aware that you are looking at them.

You don't need to see their faces.

We might hear other people, but do we really listen to what they say without immediately attaching opinions or judgements to what they are saying?

EXERCISE LISTEN TO PEOPLE WITHOUT JUDGING

Focus on your ears and LISTEN.

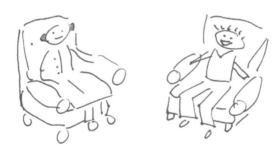

Let their words stream into you but avoid sudden reactions to what you hear.

What has been said then reaches deeper...

...and you can respond from a place where you are wiser.

Instead of worrying about reacting to what they say, you can allow yourself to receive their energy, knowledge and information.

If you are not afraid of their knowledge, their opinions, then they won't be afraid of yours.

Be present whilst walking

To make your everyday presence training even more effective, apply the techniques when you are on the move.

Try to practise this every day!

EXERCISE WALK FROM YOUR KNEES

Stop and stand for a few seconds outside your front door and…

Breathe in and sigh x 3.

Drop-a-level.

Look at your surroundings without judging.

Listen to your surroundings without judging.

Focus on a point in one knee.

Lift it forwards.

Then focus on a point in the other knee.
Lift it forwards, but not any higher than
you normally do.

YOU ARE WALKING!

Carry on looking and listening to your surroundings.

Do this and prove to yourself that you don't have to get tensed or stressed when going from A to B, even when you're in a hurry.

You can relax!!! Notice how your tempo can increase without you getting stressed or out of breath so quickly.

– Oh, I'm already here.

In fact, this is quicker!

Note It is not the knees that are important in this exercise. But by letting your knees lead when you are walking will help you to remain relaxed in the rest of the body, saving you energy.

LOOKING

- That's really nice architecture.

- I will arrive in time. I feel good.

- Just in time.

- I'm ready and present. Let's do it!

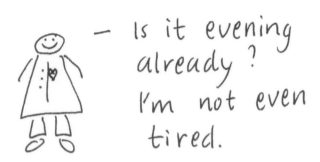

— Is it evening
already?
I'm not even
tired.

What you are doing by walking around like this is training
your instrument. Your body and your whole being is becoming
more present, calm and receptive.

You will be present where you are, wherever you are.

It is very useful to do the individual exercises whenever you find an opportunity, but I recommend that you set aside 10 minutes every day to do them all together in the following order:

EXERCISE **EVERYDAY PRESENCE TRAINING**

Stand in neutral.

Breathe in and sigh x 3.

Drop-a-level.

Look at your surroundings without judging.

Listen to your surroundings without judging.

And if possible:

Look at people without judging.

Listen to people without judging.

Walk from the knees.

By doing the exercises in this chapter
you will continue to clean and prepare your instrument.

You will ground yourself and open up a flow between you,
your surroundings and other people.

You can avoid the hard work of automatically (habitually)
needing to form an opinion about everything and everyone.

This is an excellent way of preparing for your presentation.

Chapter 4
Own your material

Learn your text and own it

Many presenters worry about remembering what to say or sing in their presentation.

For some presentations it's not important to repeat the exact words, but for some it is crucial.

It can be challenging to remain interesting i.e. in touch with the core message whilst remembering the words.

HOW you start memorising the words will have an impact on how you will be able to remember and communicate them.

Choose your material.

Sometimes the material chooses you...

Or someone else chooses it for you.

Learn your material, even if you will have a script in front of you on the day.

Love or learn to love your material.

Reflect upon Are you memorising in the head?
Many people learn their text by memorising it in their head.
Some actually build a visual memory of the text being in a
certain place on the paper.

If your presence is only in your head when learning the text,
it is likely that you will deliver it only from the head.

It is not wrong to be present in the head, but if there is little presence in the body, your presentation will be less interesting, less engaging.

If you are present in the body when learning the words you will own the material inside yourself...in your body.

To deepen the ownership of the text I recommend saying the words with a voice that is present in the body.

The next exercise will describe how you can do this.

First practise this to relax into a deeper presence in the body:

EXERCISE DCR TTT

(DROP CHIN RELAX TONGUE THROAT AND TUMMY)

Drop your chin (relax your jaw so that your mouth opens).

Relax your tongue (let the tongue rest in the floor of your mouth).

Relax your throat (gently exhale from the throat).

Relax your tummy.

Close your lips after a while, but keep your jaw relaxed.

Before you start to memorise your words,
do the next exercise once throughout all your text.

EXERCISE **ABSORB THE TEXT**

In a quiet room, with no distractions, sit upright but relaxed on a chair with your feet flat on the floor (this is a neutral position).

Have the text on a table or on your lap.

Breathe in and sigh x 3.

Drop-a-level.

DCR TTT.

Use your voice to place a relaxed, warm and gentle sound very deep down in the body.

– bla bla bla

Look at the first word and say that word using this voice, without any particular intonation.

Then look at the second word and say it with the same voice.

Continue like this throughout all your text (you don't have to do all of it in one go).

You have now started to OWN the text in the body but you still have to LEARN it and REMEMBER it...

The only way to learn anything is through repetition, so the more you do it, the better you'll get!

EXERCISE MEMORISING THE TEXT

Sit in neutral and relax as in "Own the text".

Cover the text with a blank piece of paper.

Reveal the first sentence/line. Read it aloud.

Cover it and repeat the sentence.

Reveal the first sentence to check if you remembered it correctly.

Reveal the second sentence. Read it. Cover it again.

Repeat that sentence. Check it.

Cover all the text. Repeat both sentences. Check them.

Reveal the third sentence etc. etc. etc.

Do as much as you have time for each session.

In each new session, try to start from the beginning.

You will remember more tomorrow.

More repetition

Practise the bits you know as often as you can throughout the day, whilst washing up or walking for example.

Repeat them aloud or to yourself.

To be or not to be...

Whatever you do, remember to be present in the body ...and to be present in the body, simply Drop-a-level.

Many of my students claim that Drop-a-level is "priceless" and the technique they use the most.

Chapter 5
Connect with your audience

As we established in Chapter 1:

The presentation isn't about you, it's about the audience.

Everything in this book will help you to be a presenter who the audience can relate to.

To build something beautiful...you can't have too many tools.

Here are some that will specifically help you to look at, listen to and talk to the people in the audience.

...to really connect!

Look at your audience

Do you find it challenging to look at an audience? Practise this with someone acting as an audience. Decide for one room to be "on stage" (representing the stage and the auditorium). Decide that another room will be "off stage".

EXERCISE LOOK AT YOUR AUDIENCE

Connect "off stage"

When "off stage", activate your eyes by looking at items in that space as described in "Look at your surroundings without judging" on page 37.

Make sure you look at things for real.

Connect "off stage"

Then, move "on stage" and carry on looking at things for real.

Make sure you look at the audience for real.

How confident he looks.

– wow, what a direct connection.

Listen to your audience

Reflect upon **The pillow mechanism**

Have you been a victim of the pillow mechanism?

Have you ever felt as if you are talking into a pillow?

It's like the person or the audience is not listening to you; you can't seem to get through. Perhaps they are not listening to you because YOU are not listening to them. You are the one on stage. You are in charge. You can start!

The most boring people to listen to are those who don't listen to you...

Reflect upon **The poor** listening mechanism

Two people meet:

One is not listening to the other.

And is talking all the time.

The other person soon stops hearing what the first person is saying.

He/she feels smaller and emptier and loses interest.

Neither person will end up feeling good.

This is not a meeting.

Reflect upon **The** good **listening mechanism**

Two people meet:

They listen to each other.

They are interested in each other.

They make each other feel good.

It is easy to talk.

There is a flow between them.

They both feel good.

This is a meeting.

It is the same with an audience...

Apply Technique Focus on your ears and listen to the audience, as in "Listen to people without judging" on page 45.

Result The *good* stage listening mechanism

The audience likes you
because you listen to them.
They can feel it.

This makes them feel good.
You made them feel good, so
they like you. Because they like
you...they listen to you!

You listen to each other.

You are interested in each other.

You make each other feel good.

It is easy to talk.

There is a flow between you.

This is a meeting.

Send your voice to the audience

It isn't always about the volume when you want to reach the audience with your voice.

Sometimes you don't hear what a person who shouts is saying, but you can feel clearly spoken to by a person who is whispering.

You can learn to be in control of who you are sending your voice to.

Reflect upon **The sending mechanism**

This is how it works (we actually do this all the time):

When you are saying something that you only want one person to hear, you automatically "send" only to that person and block out the other people in the room.

If you are saying something to one person, but you actually want everybody to hear, you automatically "send" your voice to everybody.

To send or not to send the voice

Practise this with someone acting as an audience.
Swap roles so that you can notice the effect.

EXERCISE STUDY NOT SENDING THE VOICE

Stand on the stage.

Use your normal speaking voice and recite a few sentences
from your text or just improvise some words.

How does it feel saying it?

How does the audience receive it?

Do the following and notice the difference!

EXERCISE SENDING THE VOICE

Stand in the same way and say the same thing with the same
voice as before.

In your mind, think that you SEND your voice to everybody's ears.

How does it feel saying it?

How does the audience receive it?

Apply Technique Think that you send the voice to every ear

Result The members of the audience feel directly spoken to

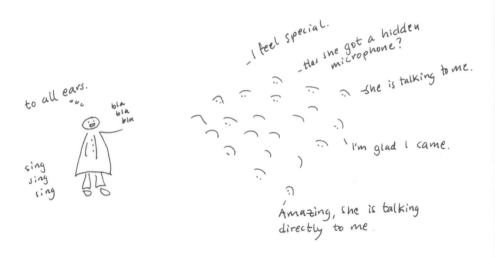

2 ears or 600 ears. It doesn't matter. It works! TRY IT!

It is so easy, yet very effective!

Chapter 6
Stage presence

Maximise your stage presence

All the exercises in this book will enhance your presence and benefit you when you are on stage (and actually in your daily life too!).

You can go a step further and develop POWERFUL stage presence where you will shine even more and really hold your audience.

I recommend that if you want to achieve captivating stage presence you should add 10 minutes to your everyday training to do the exercises in this chapter.

Or at least three times a week...

EXERCISE **PRESENCE IN THE ROOM**

Stand in neutral.

Breathe in and sigh x 3.

Drop-a-level.

Look at your surroundings without judging.

Look straight ahead at a spot on the wall.

Keep looking at that spot but open up
your peripheral vision.

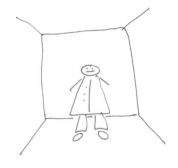

You should be able to see most of your surroundings (the ceiling,
the walls and the floor) all at once, without moving your eyes.

You can almost see behind yourself and what you can't see,
try to sense.

...to increase your awareness of what's behind you.

EXERCISE **STRENGTHEN YOUR PRESENCE**

Look and take in the whole space as you did in the previous exercise.

Hold your arms out with your palms open outwards as in the picture and feel energy flowing through your arms and hands.

Feel as if you are holding the whole room with your arms and in your hands.

Bring the arms down but feel as if you are still holding the room with them.

Feel the presence in the room.

Be present on stage before your entrance

The moments just before and whilst entering the stage can be very daunting, but that can be changed by "sending your presence".

Does that sound strange? Have a look at this:

Reflect upon
Being present
somewhere else

It is not a strange concept; we are frequently present somewhere else.

It can be useful if we learn how to master it.

Practise this with someone acting as an audience.

Decide for one room to be "on stage" (representing the stage and the auditorium). Decide that another room will be "off stage".

EXERCISE **CONTROL WHERE YOU LAY YOUR PRESENCE**

Be present on stage

Really focus on applying the "Presence in the room" technique on page 76 so that you fill the whole room with your presence.

Stay present on stage when you are leaving

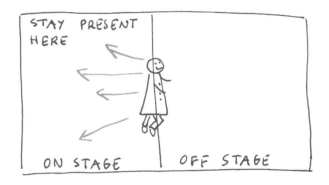

Focus on keeping your presence "on stage" whilst you now move your body "off stage".

Keep your presence on stage

And continue to focus on keeping your presence "on stage" whilst you remain "off stage".

Come back into your own presence

With your presence still there, walk back "on stage".

Notice how easy it is to enter that room and how comfortable it is to be "on stage".

This is because "you are already there".
You are already there with your presence.

Be present on stage before your entrance

Start the exercise by being "off stage".

SEND (by thinking that you are sending) your presence "on stage".

Think that you are filling that whole room with your presence.

Enter your own presence

Walk "on stage".

Enter the stage!

Chapter 7
Give and receive

Become a confident giver

We have established that the audience is more important than the presenter. The job of the presenter is to pass on information and energy. To give. Not always easy...

Reflect upon **The bad serving mechanism**

Imagine that a chef creates a nice dish but then hesitates... "They might not like it".

And he ends up not serving it.
The guests remain hungry.
What an anti-climax for the chef
and the guests.

All involved are disappointed!

So...

Don't cling on to it...

It hurts and you will get tired.

And tense.

And the poor audience will get bored and tense and wish they had stayed at home to watch telly instead.

Serve it out!

nice

The following exercises will enable you to give with confidence.

Do them with another person to really make both
the receiver and the giver feel the effect.

EXERCISE **STUDY FEAR OF GIVING**

If possible, use a real set of car keys.

Pretend that you have to let the other person borrow your car and that you are not entirely relaxed about it, because you are worried that he/she might damage it.

Give the keys to the other person and say "Here are the car keys".

How did it feel giving the keys?

How did your voice sound?

How did it feel for the other person to receive them?

Your voice is hesitant and your eyes might close a little. It doesn't feel nice to give. The receiver doesn't enjoy receiving as it is not given with confidence.

He/she can feel your reluctance.

EXERCISE **CONFIDENT GIVING**

Now do the exercise again, this time you are very happy about it and very confident that nothing bad will happen to your car.

Give the keys to the other person and say "Here are the car keys".

How did it feel giving the keys?

How did your voice sound?

How did it feel for the other person to receive the keys?

Your voice is open and your eyes open up. It feels nice to give. The receiver feels good too, as the keys are given with confidence.

EXERCISE **CONFIDENT GIVING TO AN AUDIENCE**

(no need to use car keys this time)

You are happy and confident to give.

Hold out your hand with the palm open facing upwards and give the pretend keys away.

Say "Here are the car keys". Repeat a few times.

Now, repeat without holding the arm out but remain "giving".

Say "Here are the car keys".

Now, maintain the same giving energy and say something that is more relevant to your presentation, for example:

"Welcome everybody!" I am now going to talk/sing about...

Notice how your voice is flowing and that you are giving out positive energy.

Become a confident receiver

But as a presenter, you must also receive.

You must receive the audience's energy, their laughter and other emotions and (hopefully) their applause.

Otherwise you risk disappointing/alienating your audience.

And we don't want to do that.

If you can't receive, you risk going home feeling empty...

and burnt out

job done

The audience will be ok (hopefully) but nothing special has happened.

And we want special things to happen...

EXERCISE STUDY FEAR OF RECEIVING

You are the receiver.

The other person is happy to let you borrow the car.

BUT you don't believe that you can borrow the car, it worries you.

You have fear of receiving.

The other person gives you the car keys and says
"Here are the car keys".

How does the other person feel giving the keys to you?

How do you feel receiving them?

You are not allowing yourself to receive the energy that is coming towards you. It is not nice to receive and it is disappointing for the giver.

EXERCISE **CONFIDENT RECEIVING**

You are the receiver.

The other person is happy for you to borrow the car.

You think it is great to borrow the car and so receive the keys with real confidence.

The other person gives you the car keys and says "Here are the car keys".

How does the other person feel giving the keys to you?

How do you feel receiving them?

You're allowing yourself to receive the positive energy from the giver. It is nice to receive with confidence. Both receiver AND giver are uplifted.

Result **Give and receive on stage**

How different would every show, speech and lesson be if there was a flow of energy between the presenter and the audience?

Chapter 8
On the day of your presentation

Today is the day of your presentation.

How do you feel? Is this you?

I feel sick. I am nervous.
I can't see.
Everything is blurry.
I've got a sore throat.
I've got a tummy bug.
In fact, I'm really ill.

We have to cancel!

Go with or away from the demons

Reflect upon **Are you feeding the monsters?**

It is true that the negative force inwards is strong and it will grow if you feed it.

But a lot of other things are going on, and they are also true!

It is now you need your eyes to see, your ears to listen and the ability to relax into your body.

Apply technique **Look without judging**

Switch on your eyes.

They will establish that your surroundings are without threat!

Not a wolf or dragon in sight.

Look at people without judging.

Phew – no threat!

They are harmless.

(as long as you don't judge them of course)

The overlooked important moments

Making your way to the venue on the day.

Apply technique Be present wherever you are

Apply all the techniques from the Everyday presence training on page 53.

Home

breathe in and sigh
drop-a-level
look
listen

walk from knees

on the bus

look at people without judging

Arriving at the venue can be another risky moment.

Reflect upon Bad arrival mechanism

You are judging everything and everybody.
Creating a bubble around you.

Venues and people are not always perfect. But it will have a
negative impact on you if you start judging them.

Apply technique Look and listen without judging

Result The good arrival mechanism

Look at the venue without judging.

If you have access to the space where your presentation will take place, then look at all the chairs in the auditorium.

Look at the ceiling, the floor, the walls and in any dark corners.

This will help you to "own the space".

Look at everybody around you (fellow presenters, random people and backstage crew) without judging.

Warm up this way and give yourself a chance to be:
A non-judgemental presenter.

Ego-free!

This will open up the doors to success on stage.

Waiting for your turn

Have you experienced waiting for your turn to speak, at a conference for example, and not been able to think of anything else but your presentation? Feeling as if you are in a bubble.

Apply technique **Secret activation**

Do the following actions discretely:

Breathe in and sigh x 3 (small and quiet ones)

Drop-a-level (an internal slow and gentle one)

DCR TTT (do this just for a little while)

Look and listen to people and your surroundings without judging.

If you do this, you'll be better able to participate in the event.

You might actually hear what others speak about and be able to refer to and link your speech with theirs.

Reflect upon **Are you judging your audience?**

Wow– slow down – see how busy you are!

Judging them before you have even met them!

This is likely to have a bad effect on you and consequently be picked up by the audience as soon as you enter.

If you do this, you might actually create a judgemental atmosphere.

Do not underestimate the power you have by being the one on stage.

As much as you can set a wonderful environment you can set a bad one.

Do this before your entrance:

Breathe in and sigh x 3

Drop-a-level

Look and listen without judging

Drop Chin Relax Tongue Throat and Tummy (DCR TTT)

Say this to yourself:

I want the audience to feel special

It is about them

Not me

I am serving them

Then:

Send presence to stage and auditorium

Enter the stage

Look at the audience

Listen

Be a confident giver

Send voice to all ears

Be a confident receiver

Chapter 9
After the presentation

Stay present with the audience

It is easy to think that once you have said or sung your last word that your presentation is over.

Reflect upon How do you feel afterwards?

Is this you?

- Oh no! That was a dreadful performance!

clap
clap clap

What's that sound? Applause! And you are already judging...

You are walking back on stage to receive the applause whilst feeling disappointed in yourself.

Apply technique **Stay present with your audience**

Apply "Stay present on stage when you are leaving" on page 81.

How long you should remain present with the audience depends on what kind of presentation you have done.

I recommend:
If, after a theatre-type performance you return to the stage to take your bow several times, then you should remain with the audience until your final exit.

If speaking at a wedding or seminar for example you should remain present with the audience for at least 10 minutes afterwards.

Receive feedback

Whatever kind of presentation you have performed you will, in most cases, meet the audience afterwards. You might have a Q & A time but even if you won't be talking to all of them, you will probably have a chat with somebody who saw your presentation. In all cases, apply:

Confident receiving Chapter 7

Look and Listen without judging Chapter 3

Do not judge your own presentation

Be curious about what the audience has got to say

Very rarely is any audience member interested in your opinion about the presentation anyway. They are on a journey with it now.

Evaluation time (if you need or want to)

Decide on a suitable time when you can evaluate the presentation with objectivity and creativity.

If it went really well or not so well, you need to ask "why" and "how". Praise yourself and others for what was good and come up with ideas on how to improve where needed.

Thank your colleagues and yourself afterwards.
Show them and yourself generous respect.

Result

YOU ARE GOING HOME

nice stars

nice bed

THE AUDIENCE IS GOING HOME

AND THAT IS WHY YOU HAVE BEEN CHOSEN...

TO ACT

TO SING

TO PRESENT

TO DANCE

TO PERFORM

TO TEACH

TO PREACH

TO BE

Good Luck with all your future performing, presenting, teaching and preaching.

TO BE and NOT TO DO

That is the answer

Everyday training

Stand in neutral

Breathe in and sigh x 3

Drop-a-level

DCR TTT

Look and listen to your surroundings without judging

Look and listen to people without judging

Walk from knees

On the day steps

Stand in neutral

Breathe in and sigh x 3

Drop-a-level

DCR TTT

Look and listen to your surroundings without judging

Look and listen to people without judging

Listen to the audience

Send voice to the audience

Give and receive

Stay present afterwards

Thank yourself and others

Master training

Look at your audience

Sending the voice

Presence in the room

Strengthening your presence

Control where you lay your presence

Confident giving

Confident giving to an audience

Confident receiving

EXERCISE INDEX

Thank you for your interest in my book.
I really hope that it has been of help to you.
I would be delighted to receive your feedback,
so please don't hesitate to email me on:

britt@brittforsberg.com

Thank you.